M000077632

The SEVEN LAST WORDS *of* CHRIST

Reflections by **Fr. Thomas Rosica, CSB**

Foreword by **Donald Cardinal Wuerl**

TWENTY-THIRD PUBLICATIONS

The Scripture quotations contained herein
are from the New Revised Standard Version
of the Bible, copyrighted 1989 by the Division
of Christian Education of the National Council
of the Churches of Christ in the United States
of America, and are used by permission.
All rights reserved.

Cover image: Getty Images

Interior images: Shutterstock

TWENTY-THIRD PUBLICATIONS
1 Montauk Avenue, Suite 200, New London, CT 06320
(860) 437-3012 » (800) 321-0411
www.twentythirdpublications.com

© Copyright 2017 Novalis. All rights reserved.
No part of this publication may be reproduced in any manner
without prior written permission of the publisher.
Write to the Permissions Editor.

ISBN: 978-1-62785-250-0
Library of Congress Catalog Card Number: 2016956547
Printed in Canada.

 A division of Bayard, Inc.

Dedication

For Francis, Bishop of Rome,
revolutionary of tenderness,
compassion, and normalcy,
With gratitude

Contents

Foreword by Donald Cardinal Wuerl 7

Introduction 11

Pope Francis' prayer for the conclusion of the Stations
of the Cross 15

First Word: "Father, forgive them; they do not know
what they are doing." 21

Second Word: "Today you will be with me in Paradise." 29

Third Word: "Woman, here is your son...
Here is your mother." 37

Fourth Word: "My God, my God,
why have you forsaken me?" 45

Fifth Word: "I am thirsty." 53

Sixth Word: "It is finished." 61

Seventh Word: "Father, into your hands I commend
my spirit." 67

Epilogue 75

Foreword

The Good Friday commemoration every year brings us to the foot of the cross. Here we stand in humble awe before the sign of God's love for us and Jesus' self-giving for our redemption. No one takes my life, he tells us: "I lay it down of my own accord" (John 10:18). It is here that we recognize the full meaning of Jesus' words that the Son of Man has come "to give his life a ransom" for us (Matthew 20:28).

In one of the most familiar and cherished forms of the Way of the Cross, we find this invitation to prayer: "We adore you, O Christ, and we praise you." To which we reply, "Because by your holy cross, you have redeemed the world." In this brief exchange, Saint Alphonsus of Liguori captures the essence of the article of the Creed that proclaims, Jesus Christ "Suffered under Pontius Pilate, was crucified, died and was buried."

There is much more to this statement of faith than the simple recognition that Christ died. If by his cross Christ had not redeemed us, his death would have had little meaning. With the eyes of faith, the Apostles and all of the believers after them gaze on the cross and see much more than just the instrument on which Jesus hung until he died. In writing his first Letter to the Corinthians, Saint Paul tells us that Christ sent him to preach the cross of Christ so that it not be emptied of its meaning. "For the message about the cross is foolishness to those who are perishing, but to us who are being saved it is the power of God" (1 Corinthians 1:18).

Only with the eyes of faith can we see as we stand at the foot of the cross more than failure, despair and death. As believers, as disciples of Jesus, we see so much more. What makes it possible for us to see beyond the ruined body of Jesus of Nazareth nailed to the cross to the reality of our redemption and salvation is our faith. This is the same faith that tells us that God never tires of forgiving us, even if we get tired of asking for forgiveness.

In a long-standing, prayerful tradition and pious devotion, we come together on Good Friday to be at the foot of the cross for the three hours of our redemption and to meditate on Jesus' seven last words uttered in pain. Father Thomas Rosica, CSB, CEO of Salt and Light Catholic Media Foundation, in his homilies on the words of Jesus spoken from the cross, helps us recognize the impact of those words on our lives today. Out of his recognized scriptural scholarship and his penetrating understanding of Church issues today, he takes us through those words to grasp ever more firmly their meaning.

The fact of Jesus' death is the core of the historical account and personal witness found in Matthew, Mark, Luke and John, and referred to in other parts of the New Testament. Jesus was arrested, tried, sentenced, executed by crucifixion, and was buried. The Gospel accounts are not news reports like the ones we see in newspapers or on television. The historical fact of Jesus' death must be understood through the eyes of faith. The passion narratives report an actual event, but with the primary purpose of providing its theological significance. In other words, the death of Jesus is a spiritual reality that can be interpreted only with the eyes of faith.

Standing now at the foot of the cross and reflecting on the words of Christ which, as Father Rosica points out, are not individual words but the final seven phrases that our Lord uttered as he hung on the cross, we are helped to appreciate what is happening in those three hours of Jesus' agony as he offers himself in ransom for us, and what the mystery of the cross means for each of us today in the circumstances of our time.

While the redemption Jesus won for us on the cross is the same wondrous mystery of faith in every age, the appreciation of it is found in the context of our life today. This is the age of the New Evangelization. As we take up the challenge to be evangelizing disciples today, the meditations on Jesus' last words can help us in renewing our own faith through a deeper appreciation of what Jesus has accomplished for us. At the same time, the more deeply we are enlivened in our faith, the more confident we become of its truth and the better prepared we are to be the witness that Jesus tells us we must be. Finally, nurtured and strengthened by the grace of the cross, we are prepared to step away from it and begin to share the Good News of our redemption that Christ has died, Christ has risen, and Christ will come again.

Our journey to the foot of the cross is made all the richer thanks to the insightful reflections of Father Rosica and his ability to combine scholarship with pastoral experience. It is precisely this gift that opens up for us fresh perspectives as we listen with renewed hearts and insight to the seven last words of Christ on the cross.

His Eminence Donald Cardinal Wuerl
Archbishop of Washington

September 14, 2016
Feast of the Exaltation of the Holy Cross

Introduction

The highlight of my graduate studies in Sacred Scripture at the Pontifical Biblical Institute in Rome was the great privilege of having had the late Fr. Raymond Brown, SS, as a guest professor in 1989. I took his course "The Death of the Messiah" shortly before his masterwork of the same title was published in two volumes. I remember vividly Fr. Brown's lectures on the crucifixion of Jesus, and I return to the course notes and the volumes frequently for study and reflection. Fr. Brown stressed that crucifixion was a brutal form of torture that literally knocked the wind out of a human being. The weight of the body of the crucified man, suspended by the arms, caused immediate pain in the chest, paralyzing the pectoral muscles and making breathing extremely difficult. The crucified man could inhale but had great difficulty exhaling. To exhale, he had to push on his feet and straighten his legs to release the pressure exerted on his arms and chest. But the pain that this caused to his feet was excruciating because of the nails, thus causing the crucified one to stop trying to raise himself up to exhale his breath. Death usually occurred within two or three days. But when the Romans wanted to shorten the crucified man's agony, they would break his legs. Therefore unable to straighten himself with the help of his legs, the condemned man would suffocate quickly. This was the very context in which Jesus uttered his last words or phrases: when he was literally fighting for his every breath. The Scriptures tell us that soldiers broke the legs of the two thieves crucified with Jesus to quicken their deaths, but Jesus' legs were not broken because he was already dead (John 19:31-33). In this way, Scripture was fulfilled that said none of his bones would be broken (John 19:36).

The Seven Last Words of Christ refer not to individual words, but to the final seven phrases that Our Lord uttered as he hung on the cross. "Father, forgive them; for they do not know what they are doing." (Luke 23:33-34); "Today you will be with me in Paradise." (Luke 23:39-42); "Woman, here is your son... Here is your mother." (John 19:25-27); "My God, my God, why have you forsaken me?" (Matthew 27:45-46); "I am thirsty." (John 19:28); "It is finished." (John 19:29-30); "Father, into your hands I commend my spirit." (Luke 23:44-46).

These phrases were not recorded in a single Gospel, but are taken from the combined accounts of the four Gospels. As Jesus hung on the cross, he uttered words of great meaning to those who contemplate his passion and death. His last words were greatly revered and cherished by Christians and have been the subject of many books, reflections, homilies and musical settings at various moments of history. English Catholics of the late Middle Ages were especially devoted to this pious devotion of the *Seven Last Words* and passed it on in latter-day prayer books.

What do we learn from these final moments and words of the Lord? None of us likes to suffer pain. When we suffer, we become so completely absorbed with our suffering that we forget everything and everyone else around us. Despite Jesus' suffering and torment, his increasingly difficult breathing, the agony and sadness in his soul, he could not remain insensitive to the distress of those who had followed him up to Calvary. Praying for one's torturers is not human. Jesus was able to do it because of his intimate relationship with the Father. We see in the Gospels that Jesus always showed tremendous sensitivity and compassion towards those with whom he came in contact. Suspended high on a cross, the Lord even makes arrangements for the care of his mother Mary, Mary's sister, Mary Magdalene, and John, who stood at the foot of the cross.

Nailed to the cross, Jesus is the insurgent, the revolutionary of kindness, tenderness, compassion, consolation, forgiveness and care for others. From the cross, Jesus turns us outward toward people to whom we are not physically related, identifying these people as our spiritual mothers, fathers, sisters or brothers. From the cross, Jesus breaks down the barriers between people and creates this new family by the power that flows from his death for humanity. May we learn from the words, phrases and example of Jesus crucified, for he is our bridge to the heart of God.

I am very grateful to Most Reverend Peter Sartain, Archbishop of Seattle, and to Fr. Michael Ryan, Rector of St. James Cathedral, for inviting me to preach The *Tre Ore* Service and the *Seven Last Words of Christ* on Good Friday afternoon, March 25, 2016, in Seattle's Catholic Cathedral of St. James. The Holy Week Triduum spent with this vibrant faith community was a deeply moving and prayerful experience of carefully planned liturgies, rich with piety, devotion, tradition and beauty.

I also wish to thank Joseph Sinasac, Simon Appolloni and Anne Louise Mahoney of Novalis Publishing in Canada for their guidance, encouragement, collaboration and patience throughout the editorial process. My deepest gratitude to a great friend, Cardinal Donald Wuerl of Washington, for his deeply thoughtful Foreword.

Fr. Thomas Rosica, CSB
August 6, 2016
Solemnity of the Transfiguration of the Lord

The Tre Ore Ceremony begins
with Pope Francis' prayer

for the conclusion of the Stations of the Cross

on Good Friday evening 2016
at the Coliseum in Rome

O Cross of Christ, symbol of divine love and of human injustice, icon of the supreme sacrifice for love and of boundless selfishness even unto madness, instrument of death and the way of resurrection, sign of obedience and emblem of betrayal, the gallows of persecution and the banner of victory.

O Cross of Christ, today too we see you raised up in our sisters and brothers killed, burned alive, throats slit and decapitated by barbarous blades amid cowardly silence.

O Cross of Christ, today too we see you in the faces of children, of women and people, worn out and fearful, who flee from war and violence and who often only find death and many Pilates who wash their hands.

O Cross of Christ, today too we see you in those filled with knowledge and not with the spirit, scholars of death and not of life, who instead of teaching mercy and life, threaten with punishment and death, and who condemn the just.

O Cross of Christ, today too we see you in unfaithful ministers who, instead of stripping themselves of their own vain ambitions, divest even the innocent of their dignity.

O Cross of Christ, today too we see you in the hardened hearts of those who easily judge others, with hearts ready to condemn even to the point of stoning, without ever recognizing their own sins and faults.

O Cross of Christ, today too we see you in expressions of fundamentalism and in terrorist acts committed by followers of some religions which profane the name of God and which use the holy name to justify their unprecedented violence.

O Cross of Christ, today too we see you in those who wish to remove you from public places and exclude you from public life, in the name of a pagan laicism or that equality you yourself taught us.

O Cross of Christ, today too we see you in the powerful and in arms dealers who feed the cauldron of war with the innocent blood of our brothers and sisters.

O Cross of Christ, today too we see you in traitors who, for thirty pieces of silver, would consign anyone to death.

O Cross of Christ, today too we see you in thieves and corrupt officials who, instead of safeguarding the common good and morals, sell themselves in the despicable market-place of immorality.

O Cross of Christ, today too we see you in the foolish who build warehouses to store up treasures that perish, leaving Lazarus to die of hunger at their doorsteps.

O Cross of Christ, today too we see you in the destroyers of our "common home", who by their selfishness ruin the future of coming generations.

O Cross of Christ, today too we see you in the elderly who have been abandoned by their families, in the disabled and in children starving and cast-off by our egotistical and hypocritical society.

O Cross of Christ, today too we see you in the Mediterranean and Aegean Seas which have become insatiable cemeteries, reflections of our indifferent and anesthetized conscience.

O Cross of Christ, image of love without end and way of the Resurrection, today too we see you in noble and upright persons who do good without seeking praise or admiration from others.

O Cross of Christ, today too we see you in ministers who are faithful and humble, who illuminate the darkness of our lives like candles that burn freely in order to brighten the lives of the least among us.

O Cross of Christ, today too we see you in the faces of consecrated women and men – good Samaritans – who have left everything to bind up, in evangelical silence, the wounds of poverty and injustice.

O Cross of Christ, today too we see you in the merciful who have found in mercy the greatest expression of justice and faith.

O Cross of Christ, today too we see you in simple men and women who live their faith joyfully day in and day out, in filial observance of your commandments.

O Cross of Christ, today too we see you in the contrite, who in the depths of the misery of their sins, are able to cry out: Lord, remember me in your kingdom!

O Cross of Christ, today too we see you in the blessed and the saints who know how to cross the dark night of faith without ever losing trust in you and without claiming to understand your mysterious silence.

O Cross of Christ, today too we see you in families that live their vocation of married life in fidelity and fruitfulness.

O Cross of Christ, today too we see you in volunteers who generously assist those in need and the downtrodden.

O Cross of Christ, today too we see you in those persecuted for their faith who, amid their suffering, continue to offer an authentic witness to Jesus and the Gospel.

O Cross of Christ, today too we see you in those who dream, those with the heart of a child, who work to make the world a better place, ever more human and just.

In you, Holy Cross, we see God who loves even to the end, and we see the hatred of those who want to dominate, that hatred which blinds the minds and hearts of those who prefer darkness to light.

O Cross of Christ, Ark of Noah that saved humanity from the flood of sin, save us from evil and from the Evil One.

O Throne of David and seal of the divine and eternal Covenant, awaken us from the seduction of vanity! O cry of love, inspire in us a desire for God, for goodness and for light.

O Cross of Christ, teach us that the rising of the sun is more powerful than the darkness of night.

O Cross of Christ, teach us that the apparent victory of evil vanishes before the empty tomb and before the certainty of the Resurrection and the love of God which nothing can defeat, obscure or weaken. Amen!

First Word

"Father, forgive them; they do not know what they are doing."

When they came to the place that is called the Skull,
they crucified Jesus there with the criminals,
one on his right and one on his left. Then Jesus said,
"Father, forgive them; they do not know what they are doing."

Luke 23:33-34

The moment of Jesus' death in Luke's Gospel is charged with high emotion and drama. In Luke's vivid crucifixion scene, Jesus goes to his death on the cross with the two criminals surrounding him, fulfilling his own prediction at the supper table: "For I tell you, this scripture must be fulfilled in me, 'And he was counted among the lawless'" (22:37).

The dying Jesus jars us with such a sense of shame and powerlessness in this Gospel. The evangelist offers us a lexicon of abuse and humiliation: criminals, condemnation, crucifixion, nakedness, scoffing, mocking, taunting, deriding, reviling and sneering – hardly the stuff of kingship. There are no crowns here except the one of thorns. We are face to face with agony and grief, and a barrage of insults instead of hymns of exultation and praise that echoed on the Mount of Olives just a few days before.

Just as during his lifetime among them Jesus had repeatedly taught his disciples not to respond to violence with more violence and to be forgiving, in his final moments on earth he forgives the very men who had condemned him and who drive the stakes into his body [23:34]. When one of the crucified criminals joins in the chorus of derision that accompanies Jesus to his death, the other confesses his sin and asks for mercy [23:39-43].

Jesus of Nazareth is the true king, but his power is completely different. His throne is the cross. He is not a king who kills, but on the contrary gives his life. His approach to every single person, especially the weakest, defeats solitude and sin's destiny. With closeness and tenderness, God's only Son leads sinners into the space of grace and forgiveness. He offers people mercy from the cross. In the kingdom of Jesus, there is no distance between what is religious and temporal, but rather between domination and service. Jesus' kingdom is unlike the one that Pilate knows and is willingly or unwillingly part of. Pilate's kingdom, and for that matter the Roman kingdom, was one of arbitrariness, retribution, vengeance, recrimination, privileges, domination and occupation. Jesus' kingdom is built on love, service, justice, peace, forgiveness and mercy. This is Luke's recipe for authentic conversion, as Jesus promises a criminal not only forgiveness but a place at his side on the very day when his journey to God triumphantly reaches its home in paradise.

For Jesus, the cross of death has become a cross of victory: victory of life over death, of forgiveness over violence. As followers of Jesus, we have been given new life and are called to embrace this vision of love for the world. We are called to die to self-centredness so that we may rise up in compassion and service. In his moving homily in St. Peter's Square on Palm Sunday 2016, Pope Francis spoke about this heart-wrenching scene:

> He [Jesus] forgives those who are crucifying him, he opens the gates of paradise to the repentant thief and he touches the heart of the centurion. If the mystery of evil is unfathomable, then the reality of Love poured out through him is infinite, reaching even to the tomb and to hell. He takes upon himself all our pain that he may redeem it, bringing light to darkness, life to death, love to hatred. God's way of acting may seem so far removed from our own, that he was annihilated for our sake, while it seems difficult for us to even forget ourselves a little. He comes to save us; we are called to choose his way: the way of service, of giving, of forgetfulness of ourselves.

The Latin word for "mercy" (*misericordia*) derives from two words: *miseriae* for "misery"; and *cor* or *cordis*, meaning "heart." Mercy is what happens when a heart of love meets the misery or pitiful state of others and the world. When Pope Francis speaks of the Jubilee of Mercy, he writes:

> God treats us sinners, in the same way. He continually offers us His forgiveness. He helps us to welcome Him

and to be aware of our evil so as to free ourselves of it. God does not seek our condemnation, only our salvation. God does not wish to condemn anyone! … The Lord of Mercy wishes to save everyone. … The problem is letting Him enter into our heart. All the words of the prophets are an impassioned and love-filled plea for our conversion.

This moving Gospel scene of the dying and forgiving Jesus demonstrates in a particularly dramatic way the quality and extent of divine forgiveness. The sin may be terrible, but sinners are always loved. In the final moments of his life, Jesus is only doing what he has done throughout his life on page after page of the Gospels. Remember that woman caught in adultery (John 8:1-11) who was dragged before Jesus by the scribes and Pharisees in order to force him to give judgment on the basis of the Mosaic Law? Jesus' first reply to the woman's accusers, "Let anyone among you who is without sin be the first to throw a stone at her," gives us an insight into his realistic understanding of the human condition, beginning with that of his questioners, who began to drift away one by one.

We also observe Jesus' profound humanity in his treatment of the unfortunate woman, of whose sins he certainly disapproved, for he said to her, "Go your way, and from now on do not sin again." Jesus did not crush her under the weight of a condemnation without appeal. The real enemy is our attachment to sin, which can lead us to failure in our lives. Jesus forgives this poor woman so that "from now on" she will sin no more. Only divine forgiveness and divine love received with an open and sincere heart give us the strength to resist evil and "to sin no more," to let ourselves be struck by God's love so that it becomes our strength. Jesus' attitude becomes a model to follow for every community, which is called to place love and forgiveness at the centre of its life.

To recognize and bring out the sin in others means also recognizing oneself as a sinner, and in need of God's boundless mercy. To preach the Good News of the Gospel of Jesus Christ without acknowledging the necessity of profound personal conversion and the free gift of God's mercy is to deny the central Christian message of conversion.

Jesus, you were betrayed by a friend the night before you died. We betray one another, and when we are betrayed, we remain embittered and unforgiving.

Jesus, you declared blessed those who show mercy. How often we operate on a double standard of expecting mercy and not wanting to grant it. How often we prefer the strict law and order approach over that of mercy, tenderness and compassion. Many people suffer because of us and our unforgiving attitudes.

Jesus, may we learn your vocabulary and say when others hurt us, "Father, forgive them, especially when they don't know what they are saying and doing." Father, forgive us, especially when we don't know what we are saying and doing.

Blessed Oscar Romero insisted on the need for forgiveness throughout his life. As Archbishop of San Salvador, he set an example for us of the practice of forgiveness. In every tragic circumstance he encountered, Romero spoke words of forgiveness. He asked forgiveness for murderers, for the violent, for sinners, even exclaiming, "The vengeance of God is forgiveness!" Forgiveness calms minds and reconciles after a tragedy, whenever the guilty ones were willing to repent.

Let me leave you with this quote from the conclusion of Sr. Helen Prejean's bestselling book, *Dead Man Walking*. It is particularly appropriate in light of this Gospel scene, for it highlights our daily struggle for forgiveness and reconciliation that lies at the heart of the Christian life.

Sr. Helen wrote,

> Lloyd LeBlanc has told me that he would have been content with imprisonment for Patrick Sonnier [who murdered LeBlanc's son]. He went to the execution, he says, not for revenge, but hoping for an apology.

> Patrick Sonnier had not disappointed him. Before sitting in the electric chair he had said, "Mr. LeBlanc, I want to ask your forgiveness for what me and Eddie done," and Lloyd LeBlanc had nodded his head, signaling a forgiveness he had already given.

> He says that when he arrived with sheriff's deputies there in the cane field to identify his son, he had knelt by his boy – "laying down there with his two little eyes sticking out like bullets" – and prayed the Our Father. And when he came to the words: "Forgive us our trespasses as we forgive those who trespass

against us," he had not halted or equivocated, and he said, "Whoever did this, I forgive them."

But he acknowledged that it's a struggle to overcome the feelings of bitterness and revenge that well up, especially as he remembers David's birthday year by year and loses him all over again: David at 20, David at 25, David getting married, David standing at the back door with his little ones clustered around his knees, grown-up David, a man like himself, whom he will never know.

Forgiveness is never going to be easy. Each day it must be prayed for and struggled for and won.[1]

Jesus was king even on the cross, welcoming people into his kingdom and not waiting until he was enthroned in glory. He put into practice forgiveness and mercy every single day of his life, and at times it was not easy. He, too, prayed to be able to forgive and be merciful. He struggled with the temptation to bow down before the ways of the world and the powers of the evil one. He remained steadfast to the mission entrusted to him by a God who is mercy. And in the end, Jesus won. He forgave up until the bitter end. In our last moments, may we, too, be given the ability to forgive those who have wronged us, and receive from Jesus the gifts of trust, intimacy, mercy and an open door to the Father.

---

1 *Dead Man Walking* (New York: Random House, 1993), 244–45.

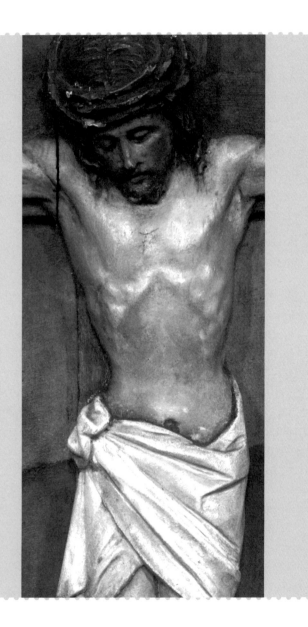

Second Word

"Today you will be with me in Paradise."

One of the criminals who were hanged there
kept deriding [Jesus] and saying,
"Are you not the Messiah? Save yourself and us!"

But the other rebuked him, saying,
"Do you not fear God, since you are under
the same sentence of condemnation?
And we indeed have been condemned justly,
for we are getting what we deserve for our deeds,
but this man has done nothing wrong." Then he said,
"Jesus, remember me when you come into your kingdom."
He replied, *Truly I tell you, today you will be
with me in Paradise.*"

Luke 23:39-43

Throughout his passion account, Luke emphasizes the mercy, compassion and healing power of Jesus (22:51; 23:43), who does not go to death lonely and deserted, but is accompanied by others who follow him on the way of the cross (23:26-31, 49). The peaceful figure of Jesus rises above the hostility and anger of the crowds and the contorted legal process. Jesus remains a true model of reconciliation, forgiveness and peace. In the midst of his own agony and trial, we realize the depths of Jesus' passion for unity: he is capable of uniting even Pilate and Herod together in friend-ship (23:12). From the cross, Luke presents Jesus forgiving his persecutors (23:34) and the dying Jesus allows even a thief to steal paradise! (23:43).

We all know this scene very well, having heard it and meditated upon it many times during our life. Close your eyes now and imagine this horrific moment. The sky has darkened and the storm is about to rip through the heavens. There are three hideous crosses planted on that ugly rock of Golgotha just outside the city walls of Jerusalem. Once again, Roman brutality results in three lives slowly slipping away before the madding and hostile crowd. Soldiers stand at the foot of the crosses jeering at the criminals. Among the witnesses are a few shocked family members, some acquaintances and maybe a few friends of the condemned criminals. Some are embracing each another; others are weeping uncontrollably. Some of the bystanders are mothers or fathers, brothers or sisters of those who are dying. Some are uttering: "This should not be happening. He is too young … he has a family … the punishment is too harsh."

Others – perhaps some who were victims of the con-demned criminals' rampages, stand there jeering, mocking and insulting those who are dying before their very eyes. Some laugh and say to the three men on the crosses: "You are getting what you deserve – you thief, you murderer, you blasphemer, you insurgent, you ugly human being." Some may even make jokes about the whole disgusting scene unfolding before their eyes. Making jokes in painfully excruciating and senseless situations sometimes eases our discomfort in a form of comic relief. Humour distances us from intimacy – from the atrocity that we are witnessing. Cracking jokes helps to suppress the nauseous feelings that rise within us. It's very easy to distract ourselves from the repulsiveness of human suffering. Others may describe this moment with *Schadenfreude*, a German word that literally means "harm-joy." It is the feeling of joy or pleasure when one sees another fail or suffer misfortune. It means to feel or express great, often malicious pleasure or self-satisfaction, at one's own success, or at another's failure.

One of the three condemned men – the one hanging on Jesus' left – found a place among the mockers and scoffers. His mind was racing desperately for a way out of this horrible mess. Everything around him was a terrible blur. He walked past the crowds of shouting, angry people and caught sight of some of his relatives who looked down upon him with fright and pity. His heart was beating so fast that it seemed ready to pop out of his chest cavity.

When he reached the top of the hill of death, that criminal was stripped, beaten again and stretched out on the wood of the cross. As the cross was hoisted up and slammed into its rocky base, pain shot up through his spine, into his arms; his legs became numb. His nakedness before the crowd was just one more humiliation. The only dose of comfort he may have received was to realize that he was not alone as he looked down upon the crowd from his new vantage point. Next to his cross were two others: two men enduring the same tragic end to their lives. Misery loves company, and this criminal was certainly not alone on the Place of the Skull.

The terror of this frightful situation is too much for the criminal to handle alone. He hears laughter and taunting below him and around him. He realizes that the crowd is making fun of the man hanging on the cross to his right – the one they call the King of the Jews or Messiah. What does this dying low-life criminal do? He joins his voice to the crowd to ridicule his neighbour on the cross. He hollers out to Jesus, "If it's true what they say about you, then save yourself! Jump down from the cross and save yourself. If you are God, save yourself and us, too! Get us all out of here right now!"

But suddenly another voice joins the cacophony. The criminal to the left of Jesus suddenly hears the criminal on the Lord's right reprimand him: "Shut up, you fool! Do you know what you are saying? The two of us are getting our just punishment for the wicked things we have done. We knew we would get the death penalty when we wreaked havoc on earth. But this guy in the middle – he is innocent. He has done nothing wrong."

What did Jesus do on earth? Why is he hanging on the cross? Because he intentionally challenged corruption in authority and blew the lid off of oppressive systems. He had women as close friends and disciples. He told parables that upset the religious establishment of his day. He cast out demons, picked grain on the Sabbath, touched people with flows of blood, visited Jewish cemeteries to seek out and heal the living dead chained to unclean tombs, and raised the dead to life. He flung furniture down the steps of the Temple when people turned it into an emporium, and he warned people about judging others.

The one hanging on the cross in the middle proclaimed the Kingdom of God and reminded people that Paradise was theirs for the asking. The Greek word for paradise is *paradisio*. It refers to the Garden of Eden – a state of delight – a place where all things were just, fair, equal and whole. It was a place of true shalom.

Then the criminal on the right blurts out amid the name calling, "Jesus, remember me when you come into your kingdom." Jesus turns his head to the thief on his right and sees that he understands Jesus, he gets it. The thief on the right realizes that Jesus has been wrongly sentenced to death because he spent his life seeking peace, justice, wholeness, holiness, shalom. Jesus was innocent of criminal behaviour and bears no shame or guilt for all he did during his lifetime, unlike the two thugs dying with him on Calvary. And then Jesus startles the thief on his right, the one whom tradition has named "Dismas" or "the dying one." Jesus tells him, "Today, you will be with me in paradise."

"*Today* you accept me as Lord of your life and are willing to stand with me even in this anguish."

"*Today*, I want you with me ... not tomorrow when you truly repent of all the evil you have wreaked upon others, or in three years after you have come to your senses and have served your time in a prison dungeon. I want you with me *today*."

"*Today*, I want you with me, because you have understood me."

During his homily at the Chrism Mass at the Vatican on Holy Thursday morning of 2016, Pope Francis reminded the clergy of his diocese,

> God does not only forgive incalculable debts, as he does to that servant who begs for mercy but is then miserly to his own debtor; he also enables us to move directly from the most shameful disgrace to the highest dignity without any intermediary stages. The Lord allows the forgiven woman to wash his feet with her tears. As soon as Simon confesses his sin and begs Jesus to send him away, the Lord raises him to be a fisher of men. We, however, tend to separate these two attitudes: when we are ashamed of our sins, we hide ourselves and walk around with our heads down, like Adam and Eve; and when we are raised up to some dignity, we try to cover up our sins and take pleasure in being seen, almost showing off. Our response to God's superabundant forgiveness should be always to preserve that healthy tension between a dignified shame and a shamed dignity.

One of the most excruciating experiences in life is to be left out, to be unwanted. How could we not think that the thief on the cross did not know the pain of rejection? We have his own admission that he deserved execution. He, too, was most likely an abandoned and unloved man, one who was also abused, a person whose life of crime reflected a loveless, unloved life. When someone lives life believing that no one would want anything to do with them, that person is prone to do bad things.

Can you imagine this criminal's shocked reaction when Jesus looked him in the eye and said, "Today, you will be with me." "You and me? A king and a terrible criminal? A saviour of the world and the scum of the earth … in paradise together? Why would Jesus want to spend time with me?"

Thankfully, Dismas experienced love, mercy and forgiveness just before he died. While it is regrettable that this criminal did not experience this love until those final moments, at least he met mercy in the flesh, hanging on the cross next to him as the two prepared to close their eyes on a violent world. After a lifetime of abuse, crime and deception, the man crucified with Jesus was extricated from the vortex of evil of the other criminals, removed from the mob hostility that was aimed at Jesus. This criminal decided to take a bold step of faith. After a lifetime of rejection, deception and violence, Dismas died in peace and entered paradise with Jesus at his side.

Here is the clincher for us: the grace, forgiveness and mercy offered to a hardened criminal on Golgotha are there for us, too. All we have to do is admit our own wretchedness, look at Jesus on the cross and ask him to remember us in our own misery, sadness and solitude. And Jesus will respond to us, too: "Today, you will be with me." Today.

Third Word

"Woman, here is your son ... Here is your mother."

Meanwhile, standing near the cross of Jesus were
his mother, and his mother's sister,
Mary the wife of Clopas, and Mary Magdalene.
When Jesus saw his mother and the disciple
whom he loved standing beside her,
he said to his mother, *"Woman, here is your son."*

Then he said to the disciple, *"Here is your mother."*

And from that hour the disciple took her
into his own home.

John 19:25-27

According to the evangelist John, there are five people at the foot of the cross, of whom the most prominent are the mother of Jesus and the beloved disciple, two figures whose names are not given. These two people are historical figures, but it is clear that John is interested in them for symbolic and theological reasons. This beloved disciple who is venerated by John's community more than any disciple of Jesus, even Peter, leader of the Twelve, is left nameless, because he is to serve as a model for all those whom Jesus loves.

John is particularly interested in Jesus' words to his mother and to the beloved disciple. Is Jesus' filial concern the main theme of this profound moment in the Fourth Gospel? Are we dealing with a historical and logistical question pertaining to the immediate departure of both the beloved disciple and the mother of Jesus from Calvary even before Jesus died? Should we understand "and from that hour" to mean that Jesus died on the cross with not one of his own with him at that final moment? Or should we understand the expression "and from that hour" as an indication of the perpetuity of the disciple's care for the mother of Jesus? Why is the mother referred to only as "woman"? Can we assume that she was well known among Christians and would not have to be named? Finally, why did Jesus wait until the last moment, when he could hardly speak, to provide for the future of his mother and her care by his closest friend?

The precise meaning of this incident is difficult to determine. At Calvary, the mother of the Lord experienced the full responsibility of her "yes" spoken to an angel in Nazareth years before. Before he dies, Jesus commits his beloved disciple to his mother's care and his mother to that disciple's care. "Here is your son!" "Here is your mother!" In his last moments on earth, Jesus is concerned, not with his own condition, but with the accomplishment of his mission and with the welfare of those he leaves behind. Mary's spiritual maternity begins at the foot of the cross. In the disciple who has been entrusted to her, Mary not only sees a dear friend of her Son, but all disciples of Jesus who have now become her children in a radically new way. This new People of God is really the Church, and Mary is the Church in her maternal role of welcoming God's word and God's people as her own.

The beloved disciple welcomed the mother of Jesus among his own, into his own community, into his most precious possessions, because he was able to recognize in this woman her great dignity in the community of believers and in the story of salvation. Not only did he welcome her as mother, but she welcomed him as son. This beloved disciple therefore became a true brother of the one hanging on the cross.

Throughout the Scriptures we find four distinct images of the communion of saints, of holy men and women. The first group is found at Bethany, in the home of Mary, Martha and Lazarus (Luke 10:38-42; John 11:1-6; 12:1-8) and represents the smallest, most intimate form of communion: a group of friends who lived in a friendly and loving environment and didn't need to defend themselves from others. They mutually accepted and loved one another. Jesus cherished his time with them, and the two sisters are deeply grateful to the Lord for raising their brother, Lazarus, from the dead. Lazarus, in his turn, brings many to admire Jesus.

The second group of holy men and women is the larger group made up of many Jews who run to see Jesus and Lazarus (John 11:26, 42; 11:45-48; 12:9-11). Such a group is a very imperfect communion of saints. Perhaps they come together for cultural or religious interests. They sincerely desire to be together, but they do so with such little faith. Many are part of such a group out of curiosity.

I cannot help but think here of the many Christians today who are deeply caught up in the sensational, in the signs and wonders, in apparitions and heavenly manifestations of Mary, of her Son, while at the same time forgetting that Christianity is best lived in the daily act of faith and service to the poor. They have not yet been able to recognize the presence of God within our history, and constantly seek him through the spectacular, through other-worldly manifestations.

The third group of the communion of saints is that of the great multitude of men and women who sing the praises of the Lord (John 12:9-15; 9:1-16; Revelation 7:4-12). This is the group that welcomed Jesus triumphantly into Jerusalem and celebrated the presence of the anointed one in their midst. The people hailed Jesus in a manner befitting a king. But he wasn't deceived by them. As he listened to their shouts, in many of them he heard the sounds of opportunism that later would demand his crucifixion. Palm Sunday's triumphal procession leads directly to Golgotha.

Did you ever stop to wonder how many members of such a group who sang "Hosanna" one day screamed, "Crucify him!" several days later? Though the Palm Sunday group is triumphal, its members may not all have the same clear agenda, the same goals and desires for the community of believers. Nevertheless, they are able to celebrate and rejoice together. Even such unholy jubilation can foreshadow redemption later on!

John also presents us with a corrected image of the large group in the Book of Revelation. We hear about a multitude so large that "no one was able to count their number," and are told that they sang the hymn of the Lamb who was slain (Revelation 7:9). These three groups presented in chapter 12 of John's Gospel and the Book of Revelation are representative of the Church at different moments of her journey. They are all valid images, but not perfect.

This small seed group of the communion of saints is found in this scene at the foot of the cross in the Fourth Gospel: the crucified Jesus, with Mary and John standing near the cross. It is the first real communion of holy people gathered around holy things: the cross of Jesus and the Holy Spirit realize the communion of saints in its fullest sense. This small group gathered at the cross must always be understood together with the immense Messianic people. And Mary is always with us, either at the beginning of the little seed or in the moment of celebration of the great people.

This is the story of Holy Week: a story of human communities welcoming the Lord and Saviour into their midst; a story of humanity and warmth, comfort and consolation in the midst of death, watching and waiting, hoping and praying, dying and rising, mercy and tenderness. How often do we strip our churches and structures of humanity, warmth and kindness because we fear these gestures and are afraid of each other? We allow ourselves to get caught up with perfection and heartless professionalism, details and rubrics, rather than with real human beings with all their weaknesses and inconsistencies. We forget that the very origin of the Church was Calvary, a true conception and birth in interpersonal communion, mutual acceptance, compassion and consolation that hold the community together. Nailed to the cross, Jesus is the insurgent revolutionary of kindness, tenderness, compassion, consolation, forgiveness and care for others. He is our pontifex, our bridge, to the heart of God.

On March 13, 2013, in the Sistine Chapel, another revolutionary was elected to follow in Jesus' and Peter's footsteps. The Cardinals of the Church chose the Cardinal Archbishop of a South American country, often considered to be at the ends of the earth, to lead the universal Church. There are those who delight in describing the new Pope as a bold, brazen revolutionary sent to rock the boat. Others think he has caused a massive shipwreck. But the only revolution that Pope Francis has inaugurated for the world is a revolution of tenderness, the very words he used in his Apostolic Exhortation entitled *The Joy of the Gospel*:

> ... For just as some people want a purely spiritual Christ, without flesh and without the cross, they also want their interpersonal relationships provided by sophisticated equipment, by screens and systems which can be turned on and off on command. Meanwhile, the Gospel tells us constantly to run the risk of a face-to-face encounter with others, with their physical presence which challenges us, with their pain and their pleas, with their joy which infects us in our close and continuous interaction. True faith in the incarnate Son of God is inseparable from self-giving, from membership in the community, from service,

from reconciliation with others. The Son of God, by becoming flesh, summoned us to the revolution of tenderness. (*Evangelii Gaudium*, no. 88)

Let us never forget that the community we call Church was born on Calvary, at Golgotha, a place of execution outside the city gates on a violent Friday afternoon over 2,000 years ago. The whole poignant scene is built around this mutual welcoming, especially in the face of tragedy, despair and death. It causes us as a Church to ask about our own welcoming, our own acceptance of peoples, of strangers, of refugees, about our own humanity, compassion and quality of friendship that we manifest to one another and to the world.

> *Stabat Mater dolorosa*
> *iuxta Crucem lacrimosa*
> *dum pendebat Filius.*
>
> *At the Cross her station keeping,*
> *stood the mournful Mother weeping*
> *close to Jesus to the last.*

This scene at the foot of the cross teaches us what it means to live in communion with others. It is exactly this spirit that Pope Francis spoke of on Holy Thursday evening 2016 as he washed the feet of refugees in Rome during the Mass of the Lord's Supper. The Bishop of Rome described the communicative power of concrete actions, saying that gestures of fraternity, tenderness, concord and peace among peoples of different religious and cultural traditions who truly desire peace and resolve to live as brothers and sisters is a powerful witness to a world desperately in need of such signs and gestures. From the cross, Jesus turns us outward toward people to whom we are not physically related, identifying these people as our spiritual mothers, fathers, sisters or brothers. From the cross, Jesus breaks down barriers between people and creates this new family by the power that flows from his death for humanity. May we learn from the example of Jesus, the beloved disciple and the mother of the Lord on Calvary, imitate their mutual welcome, and become true brothers and sisters of the one hanging on the cross.

Fourth Word

"My God, my God, why have you forsaken me?"

From noon on, darkness came over the whole land
until three in the afternoon.

And about three o'clock Jesus cried with a loud voice,
"Eli, Eli, lema sabachthani?" that is,
"My God, my God, why have you forsaken me?"

Matthew 27:45-46

While most people focus on the Lord's passion from noon to 3:00 p.m. on that fateful Friday, the evangelist Mark writes that Christ's time on the cross began three hours earlier, at 9:00 a.m., when he was nailed to the cross. Christ's first three hours on the cross were marked by the delusion of those present: passersby deriding him, and even those crucified with him insulting him.

The second three hours that Christ spent on the cross were characterized by silence and darkness and God's seeming deafness to the pleas and cries of his Son. We learn in the Lord's retreating and passing how vast a person he was among us. Our memories of what he was like before the retreat or departure become suffused with the profound weight of post-mortem insight. Perhaps, historically, Jesus died more as he does in Mark and Matthew than he does in Luke or John. Perhaps he cried out, "*Eli, eli, lema sabachthani ... My God, my God, why have you forsaken me?*" rather than "*Into your hands, I commend my spirit*" or "*It is finished.*" Still, Christians cannot help seeing the story of his death in the context of who we believe him to be, of who we know him to be.

We should not be surprised that Jesus would seize upon Psalm 22 as an expression of what he was experiencing on the cross and why he was there. Psalm 22 is a lament that is unusual in structure and in intensity of feeling. The psalmist's present distress is contrasted with God's past mercy. This psalm is important in the New Testament. Its opening words occur on the lips of the crucified Jesus (Mark 15:34; Matthew 27:46), and several other verses are quoted, or at least alluded to, in the accounts of Jesus' passion (Matthew 27:35, 43; John 19:24). Matthew's and Mark's Gospels do not hesitate to show Jesus in the utter agony of feeling forsaken as he faces a terrible death. In these Gospels also, Jesus began the journey of the passion with an anguished prayer, "Abba, Father, for you all things are possible; remove this cup from me; yet, not what I want, but what you want" (Mark 14:35-36; Matthew 26:39).

Jesus hung on the cross in the presence of mockers (Psalm 22:7; Matthew 27:39) who taunted him with the un-likelihood that God would deliver him (Psalm 22:8; Matthew 27:43; Luke 23:35) and others who cast lots for his garments (Psalm 22:18), a fact noted by all of the Gospel writers. He was fully aware that this was the moment for which he had come among us. Insulted by various categories of people, surrounded by a darkness covering everything, at the very moment in which he is facing death, Jesus' cry shows that along with his burden of suffering and death, he experiences the abandonment and seeming deafness of God. Jesus' cry to the Father from the cross was not immediately understood by those nearby. Some thought he was calling Elijah, asking the prophet to prolong his life, but Jesus was quoting Psalm 22, which affirms God's presence among his people. Jesus prays this psalm with the awareness of the Father's presence.

Many ask how an omnipotent God could not intervene to spare his own Son. We must realize that Jesus' cry is not a cry for help, but rather a prayer for his people and all peoples. By citing the opening verse of Psalm 22, Jesus was inviting all to understand his divine mission and his intense struggle as the God-man. "My God, my God, why have you forsaken me?" *"Eli, Eli, lema sabachthani?"* Certain similarities and dissimilarities exist between David's experience and Christ's. Like David, and even more than David, Jesus understood what it meant to be eternally forsaken of God. As the holy, sinless Son of the Most High, he must have felt that in an infinitely deeper way than sinful human beings can ever know.

The haunting, burning question remains: How is the God of Abraham, Isaac and Jacob present in the midst of such terror, destruction and loss? Is the answer of suffering, tragedy and loss not wrapped up in that other mystery of God's own suffering in the suffering of his Son? Whose innocence was violated. Who was also separated from his people. Who also proved to be no match for the brutality of the state. Who lifted up his hands, who stretched out his arms of love on the hard wood of the cross, that everyone might come within the reach of his loving, saving embrace?

Though the darkness enveloped people on that fateful afternoon, even in such moments of darkness God is present. In the Sacred Scriptures, darkness is a sign of the presence and action of evil, but it can also express a mysterious divine action. And it would be out of this darkness that Christ would emerge to bring life through his act of love.

For human beings, death is dark and scary and real. Even though as Christians we believe and trust in God, death can cause anxiety and anguish. Jesus does not bring us deliverance *from* death but deliverance *through* death. We do not suffer death alone. We live in a culture that, in many ways, is death-denying; it is afraid to take a clear look at the fact and the meaning of mortality. The cry of the psalmist is a profoundly human one. Jesus has made the psalmist's cry his own – and in so doing, has made it our own cry.

Jesus suffered and died because of his fidelity to God's will in his life. Jesus' preaching was good news for the poor; he ate with publicans and sinners. Many, including both political and religious leaders, found this offensive and threatening. If we show fidelity to the teaching and example of Jesus, we can face similar reactions. We may not face actual death. But we can face opposition and mockery in lesser, more subtle ways that are still painful. The psalmist's words were certainly fulfilled in the life of Jesus: "All who see me mock at me; …

they shake their heads" (Psalm 22:7). And they find echo and fulfillment in all those who choose to follow Jesus.

Both Matthew and Mark show us the human Jesus who entered fully into our human condition. There is no sentimental piety in their accounts of Jesus' death. The point is not that we can enter into Jesus' cry, but that Jesus has entered into ours. God is near, even though it may seem like he does not hear people's prayers or has abandoned his flock.

While Psalm 22 ends with hope and praise, those are not the words on Jesus' lips. Although there are no certain references in the New Testament to the second part of Psalm 22 (the hymn of praise), we do see in the Gospels that Jesus was vindicated. His Resurrection from the dead is God's stamp of approval on his life. Through Jesus' crucifixion, the meaning of death has been radically changed from the inside. Instead of representing the ultimate separation, it is now the path to greater union.

Listen to the second part of Psalm 22:

> I will tell of your name to my brothers and sisters;
>   in the midst of the congregation I will praise you:
> You who fear the LORD, PRAISE HIM!
>   All you offspring of Jacob, glorify him;
>   stand in awe of him, all you offspring of Israel!
> For he did not despise or abhor
>   the affliction of the afflicted,
> he did not hide his face from me,
>   but heard when I cried to him.

From you comes my praise in the great
  congregation;
  my vows I will pay before those who fear him.
 The poor shall eat and be satisfied;
  those who seek him shall praise the LORD.
  May your hearts live for ever!

All the ends of the earth shall remember
  and turn to the LORD,
and all the families of the nations
  shall worship before him.
 For dominion belongs to the LORD,
  and he rules over the nations.

To him, indeed, shall all who sleep in the earth bow
  down;
  before him shall bow all who go down to the dust,
  and I shall live for him.
Posterity shall serve him;
  future generations will be told about the Lord,
  and proclaim his deliverance to a people yet unborn,
  saying that he has done it.

At the end of Psalm 22, as in the Gospels, the circle of praise should go out to embrace the whole world. It is a vision of inclusiveness that breaks down all the barriers that we, as humans, are all too eager to set up. The death of Christ points us forward to the day when God's kingdom will be all in all. Faced with difficult and painful situations, when God seems not to hear us, we must not be afraid to give him all the weight we carry in our hearts; we should not be afraid to cry out to him about our suffering. Do we understand this? Can we imagine Jesus' feelings of isolation? Have we felt abandoned in suffering, or have we abandoned our loved ones in their pain and suffering? Do we ever make the psalmist's and Jesus' words our own: "My God, my God, why have you forsaken me?"

Shortly after his election to the See of Peter on April 19, 2005, Pope Benedict XVI spoke penetrating words that have remained with me every since. He reminded us of the message of hope that God is, and always has been, at work in human history, and that ultimately the power of love and good will overcome evil, just as eternal life conquers death. He said:

> History is not in the hands of dark forces, of chance, or of merely human choices. The Lord, supreme arbiter of historical events, rises above the discharge of evil energies, the vehement onslaught of Satan, the emergence of plagues and wickedness. He knowingly guides history to the dawn of the new heaven and the new earth....[2]

Jesus takes upon himself not only the suffering of his people, but also that of all men and women oppressed by evil. He takes all this to the heart of God in the certainty that his cry will be heard in the Resurrection. His is a suffering in communion with us and for us; it derives from love and carries within itself redemption and the victory of love for humanity.

---

2   Pope Benedict XVI, General Audience of May 11, 2005.

Fifth Word

"I am thirsty."

After this, when Jesus knew that all was now finished,
he said (in order to fulfil the scripture),
"*I am thirsty.*"

John 19:28

Deep within each person, created in the image and
likeness of God, is the very desire for the Creator in
whose image we were made. This desire is evoked
by the words of the psalmist: "As a deer longs for flowing
streams, so my soul longs for you, O God. My soul thirsts
for God, for the living God. When shall I come and behold
the face of God?" (Psalm 42:1-2). When we cease to thirst
for the living God, our faith risks becoming a habit; it risks
being extinguished, like a fire that is not fed. It risks becoming meaningless.

The theme of thirsting appears throughout the Scriptures
– and, in a very particular way, early on in John's Gospel during Jesus' powerful encounter at high noon with the woman
of Samaria. In that provocative scene, Jesus' thirst was not so
much for water, but for the encounter with a parched soul.
Jesus needed to encounter the Samaritan woman in order

to open her heart: he asks for a drink so as to bring to light her own thirst. The example of the Samaritan woman invites us to exclaim, "Jesus, give me a drink that will quench my thirst forever."

At the climax of the passion under the burning midday sun, stretched out on the cross, Jesus called out, "I am thirsty" (John 19:28). According to custom, he was offered sour wine, which was commonly found among the poor and could also be described as vinegar: it was considered thirst-quenching. Jesus declined to drink it: he wanted to endure his suffering consciously (Mark 15:23). This scene on the cross transcends the hour of Jesus' death. On the one hand, the account is factual: we have the thirst of the crucified Jesus and the sour drink that the soldiers customarily gave in such cases. On the other hand, we hear an echo of Psalm 69, in which the victim laments, "for my thirst they gave me vinegar to drink" (v. 21). It is not only Israel, but the Church, we ourselves who repeatedly respond to God's bountiful love with "I am thirsty": this cry of Jesus is addressed to every single person.

How could I possibly speak of Jesus' words "I am thirsty" without mentioning one who took these words to heart: Blessed Teresa of Calcutta? During my years of graduate studies in Scripture at the Biblical Institute in Rome in the late 1980s, I had the privilege of teaching the novices of the Missionaries of Charity in their formation house in Rome. On each occasion, I joined them for Eucharistic adoration and mass in their chapel that was located in a Gypsy camp in the shantytown of Tor Fiscale on the outskirts of Rome. Mother Teresa was often present for those celebrations.

Once, during Lent 1988, following mass with the sisters, Mother Teresa met me in the sacristy to thank me for my service to her sisters. I asked her why those words "I THIRST" were on the wall of the chapel. At that time, I thought they had been placed there for the liturgical season of Lent. Mother Teresa took my hand and told me quite firmly that those words are found in every convent chapel of her order – taken from Jesus' words from the cross in John's Gospel. I distinctly remember her saying to me, "They serve as a constant reminder of the purpose of the Missionaries of Charity. They remind us what an MC is here for: to quench the thirst of Jesus for souls, for love, for kindness, for compassion, for delicate love."

When visiting any convent chapel of the Missionaries of Charity – the religious order she founded – one is immediately struck by the simplicity and austerity of the sacred space. There are no chairs, pews or kneelers. The sisters take off their shoes before entering the chapel and sit or kneel on the bare floor. Typically, there are no ornate pieces of religious art – just a gold tabernacle behind the altar and a statue of Our Lady near the altar. However, the image that stands out most in every MC chapel I have visited, in various parts of the world, is the large crucifix behind the altar and the stark words painted in bold, black capital letters on the wall alongside it: "I THIRST."

Ever since her call in 1946 to leave the Loreto Sisters in India and serve the poorest of the poor in a new community, Mother Teresa insisted that the Missionaries of Charity were founded "to satiate the thirst of Jesus," and she included this statement in the founding Rules for her religious order: "The General End of the Missionaries of Charity is to satiate the thirst of Jesus Christ on the Cross for Love and Souls."

What exactly does it mean "to satiate the thirst of Jesus"? Until we know deep inside that Jesus thirsts for us, we cannot fathom who he wants to be for us, for you and for me. What specifically is Jesus thirsting for in us? Mother Teresa saw Jesus' "I am thirsty," or "I thirst," as a very personal statement spoken to each individual today, at every moment. And she said Jesus is constantly awaiting our response to his thirst. Near the end of her life, in a letter to all of the Missionaries of Charity, she made a passionate appeal to her sisters to draw closer to the thirst of Jesus and take his statement "I thirst" more seriously in their daily lives. Mother Teresa made Jesus' statement "I thirst" so personal that she told her sisters to imagine Jesus saying those words directly to them. She even encouraged them to put their own name before "I thirst" and hear Jesus saying those very words to each of them.

On March 4, 2016, four Missionaries of Charity – Sisters Anselm, Marguerite, Judit and Reginette – were massacred in Aden, Yemen, in the nursing home where they cared for the destitute poor, most of whom were Muslims. It was an act of senseless and diabolical violence. How many times did those sisters hear the words of Jesus: "Anselm, I thirst for you!" "Marguerite, I thirst for you!" "Judit, I thirst for you!" "Reginette, I thirst for you!" In the end, these four Missionaries of Charity and the twelve lay co-workers with them gave the gift of their very lives, serving Jesus in the poorest of the poor. Because they thirsted for God and quenched the thirst of Jesus, they were brutally murdered and their skulls were smashed by their killers.

When suffering persons in Yemen, Syria, Iraq, Gaza, Ethiopia, India or Sudan experienced torturing thirst, Mother Teresa and her sisters would quickly bring water to satiate the thirst of the people they served. Mother Teresa and her sisters desired to satiate Jesus' thirst by promptly responding to his will, by making sacrifices for him, by loving him in the people they serve and by entrusting their entire lives to the hands of God.

We may not be able to travel to the places where Mother Teresa's sisters minister and work with the destitute poor, but can begin to satiate God's thirst for our love by being generous with him with our time, by giving him attention throughout our day, by spending more of our lives with him in prayer. Many of us, however, are hesitant to do so. We are afraid to entrust ourselves totally to him. We cling to our own plans. Meanwhile, Jesus waits for our response as he continuously says to us, "I am thirsty."

Even though Jesus no longer needs to take up his cross and walk toward Calvary, today – in me, in others – Jesus continues to endure his passion. The small child, the hungry child who eats his bread crumb by crumb because he is afraid of running out of bread before running out of hunger – that is the first station of the cross. In our way of the cross we see Jesus, poor and hungry, enduring his own falls. Are we there to offer him our help? Are we there with our sacrifices, with our piece of bread, of real bread? Are we there to share the suffering of others? Or are we rather like the proud man who crosses over to the other side of the street, glancing at the one in need yet continuing on our way because of our business, our officiousness or our fear?

Jesus thirsts for us to speak out when we see the cross raised up in our sisters and brothers killed amid our cowardly silence. And we remain silent out of political correctness or fear of guilt by association.

Jesus thirsts for us to embrace children, women and men who are worn out and fearful, who flee from war and violence and often only find death and many Pontius Pilates who wash their hands of the vulnerable.

Jesus thirsts for us to unlock the doors of our minds and hearts, especially when we pretend to be filled with knowledge and not with the Spirit, when we have become scholars of death and not of life, who instead of teaching mercy and life threaten with punishment and death, and who condemn the just.

Jesus thirsts for us to be merciful when we are so often judgmental of others and pick up stones to throw at them and crush them without ever recognizing our own sins and faults.

Jesus thirsts for us to speak out and take action when we see public officials who try to erase the Christian memory and exclude the Gospel and the cross from public life in the name of a pagan laicism.

When Jesus breathed his last, he both handed his spirit back to the Father and handed on the Holy Spirit to the

Church. The water that flowed from Jesus' pierced side symbolizes the Spirit made available to humanity because Jesus had now been glorified in the "lifting up" on the cross (John 19:34; 7:39; 12:32). His blood is a symbol of the redeeming work of the cross. Moreover, in this water and blood, the early Fathers of the Church saw allusions to the life-giving Sacraments of Baptism and the Eucharist.

Jesus thirsts for us. He longs for us and desires to meet us at the high noons of our life to quench our thirsts. May we always thirst for him and for the life-giving water that he alone can give. Let us never be afraid to allow this water to wash over us, cleanse us, purify us and send us out on mission to feed the hunger and quench the thirst of the human family.

Sixth Word

"It is finished."

A jar full of sour wine was standing there.
So they put a sponge full of the wine on a branch
of hyssop and held it to his mouth.
When Jesus had received the wine, he said, *"It is finished."*

John 19:29-30

Throughout his passion narrative, the evangelist John emphasizes that Jesus' death on the cross is the fulfillment of Sacred Scripture. Jesus' last words are summed up in the Greek word *tetelestai*, meaning "brought to its accomplishment"; "it has been accomplished." It connotes "completion," "arriving at the intended goal." Jesus had set out to do the will of the Father, to love his own "until the end."

Three times God used that same word in history: first, in Genesis, to describe the achievement or completion of creation; second, in the Book of Revelation, when all creation would be done away with and a new heaven and earth would be made. Between these two extremes of the beginning and the accomplished end, there was the link of these words with the final expression of Jesus from the cross. It is as though God's only Son, at this horrible moment of his life when he was stripped and humiliated, seeing all prophecies fulfilled, all foreshadowings realized, and all things done for the Redemption of the human family, uttered a cry of joy: "It is achieved." Like he has done so many times, John uses the words here with a double meaning. The word "finished" refers to the physical and temporal end of Jesus' life. But it also tells, at the same time, of the total accomplishment of the mission entrusted to him by the Father.

In Jesus' crucifixion, we see the fulfillment of an important Jewish ritual, the Day of Atonement. On that day each year, the high priest entered the inner tabernacle with an offering to atone for Israel's sins. On Golgotha, Jesus was both the victim and the great high priest. The atoning sacrifice was no longer the blood of an animal, but Jesus' own blood. No longer was it necessary for the high priest to enter into the Holy of Holies in the Jewish Temple, which was a symbol of the heavenly tabernacle. Now Jesus offered himself directly to his Father in heaven.

Bowing his head in a graceful and composed manner, the Word made Flesh hands over his life spirit to God. There is a luminous sense of serenity and strength as the Jesus of John's Gospel meets death. His death is no play-acting. John makes that point in the spear thrust that follows, but in this scene on the cross, the terror of death has been defused by love.

But what exactly does Jesus' death accomplish? For John, Good Friday is already Pentecost. On the one hand, Jesus hands his life over to God, from whom he received it. But he also hands it over to his disciples. Even the bowing of his head at the moment of death can be interpreted as a nod in their direction. Out of Jesus' death comes life for his followers. In colloquial speech today, Jesus might have said, "Mission accomplished!" "It's in your hands now!"

As we gaze on the face of the crucified Jesus today, what do we see? One who lives in the grip of anxiety, but within whom the seed of a new being will be a source of empowerment not only for us, but also for those around us! In his death, Jesus becomes for us a point of embarkation. We all know people like this: just being in their presence somehow seems to sort things out for us – it puts the pieces of our lives back together again. As one of the characters in Toni Morrison's award-winning book *Beloved* describes the effect of the woman he loves upon him: "She gather me, man. The pieces I am, she gather them and give them back to me in all the right order."

There are people in each of our lives of such depth, such substance, such solidity, that others stand on the firm ground they provide and embark on their own lives through them. This, of course, is the role that all of us who are leaders, teachers and parents hope to play for our students, our children, our flocks, though we do so with varying, incomplete success. Later in life, we may be lucky enough to find such an embarkation point in a parent, a friend, a mentor, a psychotherapist, yes, even a bishop, priest, rabbi or minister. Anything is possible! And what a privilege it is if we ourselves become the embarkation point for others.

This process, whereby people become the foundation that allows others to face the world, went on amid the horrors of the Holocaust. I remember reading a very moving story by the Jewish writer Yaffa Eliach, in her book *Hasidic Tales of the Holocaust*.[3] Eliach writes about Anna, a young woman who was stricken with typhus during the epidemic in the Bergen-Belsen concentration camp. She was terribly ill and weak, stumbling over the dead and the dying as she finally collapsed on what she thought was a hill shrouded in grey mist. The hill represented a symbol of life for Anna – she reached her final destination and collapsed atop the hill. She cried out to her father, who had been incarcerated in that camp four years earlier, and as she moved in and out of consciousness, she felt a warm hand rest on her head. She believed it to be her father's touch, as at the family's Friday Shabbat dinners. Her father seemed to be telling her not to worry, and that she would survive for a few more days, since liberation was at hand. That moment took place on the night of Wednesday, April 11, 1945. Four days later, the first British tank entered Bergen-Belsen.

Only when Anna was discharged from hospital in the British zone did she realize that the huge mound of earth where she had passed out in a delirious state was a mass grave. One of the victims buried there was her father, who had died months earlier in the concentration camp. Anna had been weeping uncontrollably on her own father's grave.

Yaffa Eliach's story of Anna makes a similar point to the theme of embarkation announced in John's Gospel. Even

3 *Hasidic Tales of the Holocaust* (New York: Vintage, 1988), 177–78.

death does not stop Anna's father from coming to her, blessing her, promising her that she will live, and encouraging her to hold on just a little while longer. Death cannot stop those significant persons in our lives from becoming embarkation points for us. Indeed, their importance may even grow. We may come to see aspects of who they were for us that we never realized when they were alive.

When such people are taken away from us so suddenly, and there is no time to say goodbye, the pain is even greater. Sometimes we soften the tragedy by saying that some people died natural deaths. They weren't shoved into gas chambers, stark naked and humiliated. They didn't die from starvation or typhus. Still, from the biblical perspective, "natural death" is a misnomer, because every death is a violation of the God-willed order for creation. One thing we often hear from survivors of the Holocaust or of other great tragedies of the past centuries, and even our century, is that they didn't have time to say a proper goodbye. Partly because guards were standing there with whips, screaming at them to keep moving. Partly because the survivors didn't know they would never see their mothers, fathers, brothers or sisters again, because they didn't know that this parting was for eternity.

Today, on this Friday that we dare to call "good," we experience another sort of communion. The various parts of this form of communion – the tragedies of Jewish history, culminating in the Holocaust, and with Jesus' death on the cross – are inextricably bound up with each other. For the death of Jesus invites us all, especially Christians and Jews, into a knowledge of our communion with one another and a recognition of the terrible brokenness of the world. Nothing and no one can ever wrench us away from that communion. Nothing can remove our sense of belonging to, participating in, and being the beneficiaries of God's saving encounter with Israel and with the broken world, which occurred in the crucifixion of Jesus, son of Israel and Son of God.

Today, as we stand grieving, huddled together on this hill of death, surrounding the most important member of our community, and hear his final words – "It is finished. It is accomplished." – we know in some strange and mysterious way that the God of Abraham, Isaac, Jacob and Jesus gathers up the broken pieces of our lives, puts them all back together, in the right order, and makes us whole again. And the world will only be healed, repaired, restored, renewed if we Christians and Jews become such points of embarkation for one another and for the world.

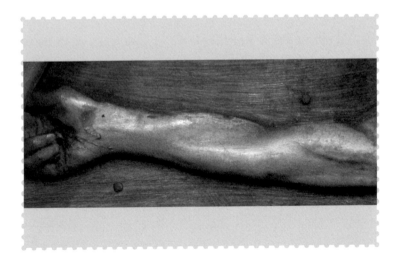

Seventh Word

"Father, into your hands
I commend my spirit."

It was now about noon, and darkness came over the whole
land until three in the afternoon, while the sun's light
failed; and the curtain of the temple was torn in two.

Then Jesus, crying out in a loud voice, said,
"Father, into your hands I commend my spirit."
Having said this, he breathed his last.

Luke 23:44-46

From the midst of the terror and violence of Calvary
comes Jesus' piercing voice, his life breath poured out
in a final prayer: "Father, into your hands I commend
my spirit" (Luke 23:46). The words are from Psalm 31 [v. 5]
and express the core of Jesus' being – his unshakable trust
in God, a trust that death itself could not destroy. Why does
Luke place the words of this psalm on Jesus' lips, and not
Psalm 22, as Matthew and Mark do? Could it be that Jesus
prayed not one but both psalms in his final moments? What
does this tell us about the piety and devotion of Luke's Jesus?

Let's go back to the beginning of Jesus' ministry in Luke's Gospel. On the banks of the Jordan River, he heard these words from heaven: "You are my Son, the beloved" (Luke 3:22). Throughout this entire Gospel, Jesus lives and dies in intimate relationship with his beloved Father. Throughout the Gospel, he remains faithful to his identity. In the Sermon on the Mount on a Galilean hillside, Jesus exclaims, "Blessed are the peacemakers, for they will be called children of God" (Matthew 5:9). "Love your enemies … so that you may be children of your Father in heaven; for he makes his sun rise on the evil and on the good, and sends rain on the righteous and on the unrighteous" (Matthew 5:44-45). From the desert to the cross, Jesus resisted the temptation to deny his true identity, to doubt God. He trusted in God, and in the end surrendered to God. He wants us to do the same. With his dying breath in Luke's account, Jesus surrenders himself unconditionally to God. "Father, into your hands I commend my spirit."

The Gospel invites us to claim our true identities as sons and daughters of God. As we prepare for our own deaths, we may wish to make Jesus' words our own, and cultivate that interior attitude of unconditional surrender to God. If we want to be able to utter them on the day of our own deaths, we need to start saying them now, and live our way into that loving surrender of our lives to God.

It is said that the final moments of one's life provide a snapshot of our entire life. Jesus' spiritual life was steeped in the psalms of David, the prayer book of ancient Israel. The Son of God was a descendant of David and was hailed on Palm Sunday as the Son of David (Matthew 21:9). When Jesus prayed Psalm 31 from the cross, he was expressing the leitmotif of his entire life: tremendous trust in God in the midst of agony and suffering, and even seeming abandonment. In his dying moments, Jesus reached into the depths of his experience for the words of his ancestor David. In this extraordinary moment of intimacy, he referred to Psalm 31:5, "Into your hand I commit my spirit," because he implicitly trusted in God. The two belong together: trust nurtured by intimacy; intimacy nurtured by trust. The intimate word Jesus added to the words of David was *Father*. "*Father*, into your hands I commend my spirit."

Just before Jesus' final expression of trust, the evangelist Luke tells us that the heavy curtain of the temple was torn in two from top to bottom. People have interpreted this event in many different ways, but this detail is a clear indicator of a newly opened avenue to God. The structures of worship can be either obstacles or bridges. They both separate worshippers from and connect worshippers to the divine. But in the tearing of the temple veil we see destroyed the formal separation between worshippers and the One who is adored, as Jesus himself provides free and open access. In Jesus crucified, we behold the one who is indeed our Way, our Truth and our Life. In Jesus' death, we experience God's mercy for humanity.

The opposite of mercy is not justice but vengeance. Jesus did not oppose mercy to justice but to the law of retaliation: "eye for eye, tooth for tooth" (Exodus 21:24). In forgiving sinners, God is renouncing not justice but vengeance; he does not desire the death of a sinner but wants the sinner to convert and live (see Ezekiel 18:23). On the cross, Jesus did not ask his Father for vengeance. He entrusted himself to the hands of a loving Father, forgave criminals, absorbed the evil, wretchedness and sin of the human condition, and bowed his head in peace.

The cross of Christ amassed all the arrows of evil: hatred, violence, injustice, pain, humiliation – everything that is suffered by the poor, the vulnerable, the oppressed, the exploited, the marginalized and the disgraced in our world. However, we can rest assured that for all who are crucified in this life, as in the case of Christ, the Resurrection follows the cross; hatred, violence and injustice have no prospect; and the future belongs to justice, love and life. Therefore, we must journey toward this end with all the resources we have in love, faith and patience.

The words come to us with difficulty today. We are stunned and we mourn and grieve over the loss of the dearest member of our community. Let us turn to the Scriptures and make the prayers of Jesus' friends our prayers as we remember Jesus' death in Jerusalem. Perhaps we need to cry out, "Where are you, God?" "If only you had been here, our brother would not have died!" Today we are given the answer: God is hanging on a tree, in the broken body of a young man – arms outstretched to embrace us, and gently asking us to climb up onto the cross with him, and look at the world from an entirely new perspective.

Or perhaps we need to cry out for mercy, asking that he not forget us in the new Jerusalem: "Jesus, remember me when you come into your kingdom." Or maybe in the midst of our despair, we need to recognize the source of our hope and echo the words of Jesus, "Father, into your hands I commend my spirit."

And from the depth of our own darkness and shadows, we might have to pray with Cleopas and his companion on the road to Emmaus: "Stay with us, because it is almost evening and the day is now nearly over" (Luke 24:29). Or perhaps we are Peter, stunned by his master's extraordinary gentleness and patience with him, and we can only utter, "Yes, Lord; you know that I love you" (John 21:16).

Let me leave you with these words from a great pastor and shepherd of the Church who was like a meteor lighting up our night for only 33 days back in 1978. Before being elected to the See of Peter and taking the name of John Paul I, Cardinal Albino Luciani, then Patriarch of Venice, wrote a weekly column in his diocesan newspaper. The column consisted of letters to various personalities and great figures in history. One of the last letters he wrote, in great trepidation, was to Jesus. I quote from that deeply moving letter:

> At this spectacle of people rushing to a Crucifix for so many centuries and from every part of the world, a question arises: Was this only a great, beneficent man or was He a God? You Yourself gave the answer and anyone whose eyes are not veiled by prejudice but are eager for the light will accept it.
>
> When Peter proclaimed: "You are Christ, the Son of the living God," You not only accepted this confession but also rewarded it. You have always claimed

for Yourself that which the Jews reserved for God. To their scandal You forgave sins, You called Yourself master of the Sabbath, You taught with supreme authority, You declared Yourself the equal of the Father. Several times they tried to stone You as a blasphemer, because You uttered the name of God. When they finally took You and brought You before the high priest, he asked You solemnly: "Are you the Christ, the Son of the Blessed?" You answered, "I am; and you will see the Son of man sitting at the right hand of Power and coming with the clouds of heaven." You accepted even death rather than retract and deny this divine essence of yours.

I have written, but I have never before been so dissatisfied with my writing. I feel as if I had left out the greater part of what could be said of You, that I have said badly what should have been said much better. There is one comfort, however: the important thing is not that one person should write about Christ, but that many should love and imitate Christ.

And fortunately – in spite of everything – this still happens.[4]

It still happens. Whatever our words may be, there is a consolation that if we pray them with reverence, then our prayers will be heard. They never go unanswered. Jesus,

---

4 Cardinal Albino Luciani (Pope John Paul I) "To Jesus: I Write in Trepidation" in *Illustrissimi: Letters from Pope John Paul I* (Boston: Little, Brown & Company, 1978), pp. 254–55.

the great High Priest, intercedes for us and even gives us the words that are necessary when our human words fail. For it was this great High Priest who has marked us as his own through our Baptism, and today immerses us into the priesthood of his suffering. He entrusted himself to the hands of his Father and he entrusts himself to our hands, that we may bear him to the world that so badly needs his message, his presence, his mercy and forgiveness. On this day when we remember Jesus' ultimate gift to humanity, let us entrust ourselves to the hands of a merciful God. And as we make the sign of the cross, let us be mindful of that common priesthood and mission so lavishly given to each of us through Jesus' death on the cross.

"In the Name of the Father"
depending on God, we touch our minds
because we know so little
how to create a world of peace and hope.
"In the Name of the Son"
depending on God, we touch the centre of our body
to bring acceptance to the fears and pain
stemming from our own passage through death to life.
"In the Name of the Spirit"
depending on God, we embrace our heart
to remember that from the centre of the cross,
God's vulnerable heart
can bring healing and salvation to our own.

Epilogue

Each year on Good Friday, we relive the tragic chain of events of the passion of our Saviour leading to his crucifixion on Golgotha. A haunting question about this day has resounded throughout history: Where was God in the midst of the disaster on Calvary? This is a question that even Jesus the Lord cried out from the cross: "Where are you? Have you really forgotten me? Why are you deaf to the sound of my pleading?" (Psalm 22).

Good Friday shows us where God is – hanging on the cross in Jerusalem, and on the crosses throughout the world where people are betrayed by an ally, abandoned by a friend, denounced by their community, shouted at by crowds, made into a scapegoat, passed from authority to authority, physically abused, mocked and humiliated, labelled and mislabelled, stripped of their clothing and dignity, tortured and executed out of anger, violence, jealousy or hatred. The way of the cross and the words spoken from the cross continue in our world today.

During my time as Catholic chaplain at the University of Toronto's Newman Centre from 1994 to 2000, a very faithful elderly Catholic woman confided to me one Good Friday the struggles that she and her family were having with accepting the cross as the central symbol of the Christian life. The woman wept as she expressed concern about her daughter's troubled faith, and she shared with me a poem that her daughter had written about the cross.

Far from describing a lack of faith, the poem reveals the raw faith and deep love that the mystery of Good Friday and the final words of the Lord call forth from all Christians throughout the world. Here is that poem:

> "But Lord," I complained,
> "This cross is too heavy, too awkward,
> It protrudes in the front, it drags in the back,
> It slips off the side, it just does not fit,
> Lord, it cannot be for me!"
>
> "Ah, gently, gently," says He.
> "It is not the cross that needs altering,
> It is your way of carrying it."
>
> And stooping down ever so graciously,
> He, the Connoisseur of Crosses, and cross bearing,
> Adjusted mine, straightened my shoulders,
> Beckoned me to look up and to smile,
> To carry it with dignity, if not with love,
> For I was following in a great tradition.[5]

---

5 Used with permission.

Allow me to conclude these reflections by quoting the final words spoken by Pope Francis at the end of the stunning World Youth Day Stations of the Cross in Krakow's Błonia park on Friday afternoon, July 29, 2016.

> The Way of the Cross is the way of fidelity in following Jesus to the end, in the often dramatic situations of everyday life. It is a way that fears no lack of success, ostracism or solitude, because it fills our hearts with the fullness of Jesus. The Way of the Cross is the way of God's own life, his "style", which Jesus brings even to the pathways of a society at times divided, unjust and corrupt.
>
> The Way of the Cross is not an exercise in sadomasochism; the Way of the Cross alone defeats sin, evil and death, for it leads to the radiant light of Christ's resurrection and opens the horizons of a new and fuller life. It is the way of hope, the way of the future. Those who take up this way with generosity and faith give hope to the future and to humanity. Those who take up this way with generosity and faith sow seeds of hope. I want you to be sowers of hope.